My personal
CPD Record

Richard Winfield

Brefi Press
www.brefipress.com

Copyright © 2017 by Richard Winfield

All rights reserved

The right of Richard Winfield to be identified as the author of this work has been asserted by him in accordance with the Copyright, Designs and Patents Act 1988.

All rights reserved. No part of this publication may be reproduced, stored in or introduced into a retrieval system, or by any means (electrical, mechanical, photocopying, recording or otherwise) without the prior written permission of the publisher. This book is sold subject to the condition that it shall not, by way of trade or otherwise, be lent, resold, hired out, or otherwise circulated without the publisher's prior consent in any form of binding or cover other than that in which it is published and without a similar condition including this condition being imposed on the subsequent publisher.

Cover design by Chris Walker, Expressive Design.

First published in 2017 by Brefi Press

ISBN 978-0-948537-19-6

www.brefipress.com

Books by Richard Winfield

The New Directors Handbook

The NED Directors Handbook

The AIM Directors Handbook

Checklists for Directors and Boards

CPD Guides for Directors (series)

Stories from a Corporate Coach

Reflections of a Corporate Coach

Lessons from a Corporate Coach – Coaching

Lessons from a Corporate Coach – Business

www.brefipress.com

Contents

1. Introduction to your personal CPD Record 1
2. Journaling 3
3. Personal audit 4
4. IoD standards – Quick check director performance 7
5. Goal setting and review 9
   - CPD Record – September 19
   - CPD Record – October 21
   - CPD Record – November 23
   - CPD Record – December 25
   - CPD Record – January 27
   - CPD Record – February 29
   - CPD Record – March 31
   - CPD Record – April 33
   - CPD Record – May 35
   - CPD Record – June 37
   - CPD Record – July 39
   - CPD Record – August 41
6. Review and carry over 43

Brefi Group Limited

One Victoria Square
Birmingham B1 1BD

+44 (0) 121 288 3417

www.corporatedirector.co.uk

1. Introduction to your personal CPD Record

Continuing professional development is a lifelong activity to ensure that you develop your professional competence, upgrade your skills and keep yourself appraised of developments.

For directors it includes corporate governance, developments in the corporate sphere – legal, regulatory and market – and your own functional skills. These are likely to include strategy and management, and could also include finance, legal, human relations etc.

Richard Winfield

Remember: where regulation and litigation are concerned, ignorance is not an excuse.

At director level you are expected to have a broad range of skills and experience, and a high level of awareness of current affairs.

CPD covers a wide range of activities from reading a national paper and monitoring TV and radio news to attending formal courses.

Your CPD objectives can include generally developing your skills, keeping up to date with developments and targeting specific new skills and competences.

CPD is a personal journey owned and managed by you. Most professional institutions have CPD requirements, expecting you to undertake up to 30 hours CPD every year.

CPD schemes normally work on the basis of collecting points, related to the time devoted to the learning. For an activity to count towards CPD points it must be relevant to your career, contain significant intellectual or practical content and have a clear learning objective and outcome.

Many workshops and events for professionals advertise the relevant points that can be earned and might even provide a certificate of attendance/completion as evidence.

Schemes are normally trust-based but you do need to keep a record. This document has been provided for you to do this and, in addition, provides a structure for creating an effective personal development plan and following it thoughout a twelve month period.

I have chosen to design it September to August; not only does this match the academic year in the northern hemisphere but it also recognises August as the major holiday period – an excellent time for reflection and planning.

I recommend that your professional development plan should involve a mix of general and strategic objectives, and a mix of different types of activity. These typically include:

Reading:
- Books
- Newspapers and magazines, including *The Economist*
- Specialist media such as the *Harvard Business Review* and professional journals
- Newsletters and blogs

© Copyright 2017 Brefi Group Limited

Courses:
- Self-study programmes, online or DVDs
- Live workshops
- Short courses
- Professional education courses leading to relevant qualifications

Events:
- Networking event talks (not including social time)
- Conferences and exhibitions
- Webinars and podcasts
- Study visits

Activities
- Planning/research for an article or presentation in relation to business, economics, corporate governance or other subjects for the public benefit
- Providing coaching or mentoring
- Membership of a committee or working party of a professional institution, trade association etc.

The UK Institute of Directors recommends that you plan your development programme in advance, and over a reasonable period, say two years, in terms of what you wish to achieve, and the steps that you will take to do so. They suggest three questions to consider when completing your CPD record:

- How relevant was the learning to your career?
- Can you state how you will use that learning?
- Can you provide evidence of having undertaken specific learning activities?

Learning styles

Peter Honey and Alan Mumford have developed a Learning Style Questionnaire, which will help you match learning opportunities with how you learn best.

It will help you to pinpoint your learning preferences, so that you are in a better position to select learning experiences that suit your style, and learn how to benefit from other means of learning.

You can obtain a free demo at https://www.talentlens.co.uk/develop/peter-honey-learning-style-series.

Learning style	Type of learner	Learning preference
Activists	Hands on	Trial and error
Reflectors	Tell me	Briefed before proceeding
Theorists	Convince me	Clarity – Does this make sense?
Pragmatists	Show me	Likes an expert to demonstrate

The Chartered Management Institute recommends using all four styles in a cycle:
- Reflection – What are my needs or objectives?
- Planning – What am I going to do?
- Evaluation – What have I learned?
- Action – What have I done?

In addition, you should include a revision cycle in which you review recent learnings two or three times to mitigate the natural loss of memory with time; perhaps review recent entries each time you update your CPD record.

The purpose of your CPD activity is to develop your knowledge, skills, attitudes and behaviours. This is where reflection is so important. I recommend that you obtain a luxury notebook or journal in which you can record your thoughts about your learnings and their application.

Many people find that a daily journaling session is valuable and rewarding, and I include a section on journaling as a guide.

I have also included some exercises to help you determine your personal mission and ensure that your professional activities draw on your strengths and motivation.

The year starts with self analysis and goal setting, and ends with a review of achievement. This should then feed into the self analysis and goal setting in next year's record.

2. Journaling

Some of the most influential people in history have kept journals. Not only is a journal a record of your progress, it is an excellent way of raising your awareness; and keeping a private journal can be cathartic.

Journaling is a great way to organise your thinking and to get lots of ideas and topics swirling around in your head out of your brain and onto the page, where you can deal with them.

The first stage is to obtain your *luxury* notebook. Preferably with a leather binding in a series that you can add to over the years. Your journal should ideally be a physical thing. This is not an exercise for your tablet or phone. There is something creative and engaging about the physical act of writing, its pace slows you down and gives you more time for thoughts to come in. You can use coloured pens and include sketches, diagrams and Mindmaps®.

However, if you are more comfortable typing, there are lots of apps designed for the purpose.

One thing to decide at the start is whether this is to be a private journal – if so, then you are likely to be more relaxed and honest in what you write.

Journaling is not the same as keeping a diary; use this document to record activities. Your journal is a creative space in which you both record and develop your ideas.

Here are three ways that you could use one:

Daily – objectives and achievements diary

First thing or last thing, whichever works best for you. Record what you intend to achieve tomorrow/today, what you did achieve and what you learned. You should also start to note down what you are grateful for.

As well as the content these notes generate, they will train your mind to start noticing and enquiring naturally, and you will automatically raise the level of your awareness

Freewriting (stream of consciousness)

Freewriting is one of the most effective and easy forms of journaling. The idea is to write for a specified length of time (usually ten minutes), or to fill a specified number of pages, and not to stop until the timer's sounded or the pages are full. What you write about is not important — only that you write and that you do it without stopping, without thinking, without evaluating or judging what you write.

There is no need to be intimidated by an empty page. If you do not know what to write or you dry up, just write "I wonder what I should write about now; what would be most useful to think about; how can I make the best use of the this time?". Don't worry about structure, grammar or spelling – just write, and keep writing.

Analysis and evaluation

This is directly related to your CPD activity. Before you start a session set yourself some targets and then afterwards analyse and record what you have learned. Then put it into context and decide how you can apply it. Maybe identify further work, ideas to follow up or books to get hold of.

Review

Remember to take the trouble to review your writings, maybe once a week or on the first day of each month. Not only will this help embed what you have learned but it will be a great motivator to look back and realise what progress you have made.

3. Personal audit

It is useful at the beginning of every year to carry out a personal audit to review what your are, where you are and where you are going.

What do I really want?

Here are some questions I have found useful. They will help you decide where to focus your energy. If you do what you really enjoy and avoid what you don't, you will probably find that you are doing more of what you are best at, and continuously improving.

- What do I really, really enjoy? What do I truly love to do?

- What do I enjoy?

- What do I not enjoy?

- What am I really good at?

- What is important to me?

- What do I want?

Personal mission

Dr John Demartini has developed a model for developing a personal mission. I have used it and found it very useful. Keep developing it until every word feels natural and congruent – it could take several months (or a lifetime!). Then return to it on a regular basis and read it out loud to reinforce your commitment and to remind your unconscious what to look out for.

Demartini suggests that you write down what you would love to be, do and have in all seven areas of your life. Any detail you leave out is a detail that others may determine for you.

Write out a general list and then repeat the exercise for each of:

Spiritual, Mental, Vocational, Financial, Familial/Home, Social and Physical.

When you have refined what you would like to be, then turn it into a purpose statement by adding your commitment to achieve it.

The clearer your life mission, the more you will live and fulfil it. The more your secondary objectives for each of the seven areas of life align with your primary purpose, the more fulfilling your life will become.

If your written purpose is truly an expression of your highest values you will automatically feel dedicated, committed and determined to fulfil this important life mission.

When I was learning to use it Demartini gave his own general statement as an example. Here is mine: -

> **I Richard Charles Winfield hereby declare before myself, others and God that my primary purpose in life is to become whole, to make sense of the world and to be a resource to others.**
>
> **Be:** A seeker after the truth in at least the fields of management and director development, making sense of the world and interpreting it for others.
>
> **Do:** Bring joy into the world and help people grow; discover, integrate and disseminate ideas and processes that help individuals and teams in organisations achieve their potential in a congruent and ethical manner; prepared to challenge and confront received wisdom, established ideas and opinions; leveraging my value; travelling to places and cultures, both to learn and to spread appropriate knowledge and wisdom; congruent with my emotions and relationships; able to heal myself easily and naturally, aligned and balanced, healthy and fit.
>
> **Have:** Be well rewarded for my contribution and live a privileged and highly cultured life for the sake of the fulfilment of this life long quest.

Now prepare your own list. You can download a form at:

www.brefigroup.co.uk/acrobat/demartini_mission_statement.pdf

Start with the known and move to the unknown. Think outrageously and then gradually refine until you have defined exactly what you truly want.

When you have completed the exercise, decide on the top priority, most meaningful goal, objective or project in each of the seven areas of your life that you would love to have completed or accomplished by exactly one year from today. These seven can be 'beings', 'doings' or 'havings'.

Review your list daily or weekly so that you maintain a strong focus on what really matters to you and ensure that you and they a fully congruent.

Remember to review your mission statement and goals list daily or weekly so that you maintain a strong focus on what really matters to you.

360º feedback

It is very useful if you can get independent feedback from those who know you.

If you just ask people they might be inhibited by the request or feel they need to be polite. Better, would be to set them some questions or statements requiring a score of one to five. The ideal is to get a third party to manage the process – there might well be opportunities for this in an organisation as part of the annual appraisal.

You can organise an on-line individual and 360º feedback exercise at:

www.buddycoach.co.uk.

Action planning

Here are six simple questions to help you focus on what you need to do:

Where am I now?

How did I get here?

Where do I want to go?

Why do I want to go there?

What stands in my way?

What am I going to do about it?

4. IoD standards – Quick check director performance

Try these two quick checks on your performance as a director and that of your board and of individual directors. They are based on the Institute of Directors publication *Good Practice for Directors – Standards for the Board*.

Quick check director performance

- I rise above the immediate problem or situation and see the wider issue and implications.

- I am aware of the organisation's strengths and weaknesses and of the impact of the board's decisions upon them.

- I generate and recognise imaginative solutions and innovations.

- I show a readiness to take decisions, make judgements, take action and make commitments.

- I insist that sufficiently detailed and reliable information is taken account of, and reported as necessary.

- I probe the facts, challenge assumptions, identify the advantages and disadvantages of proposals, provide counter arguments, and ensure discussions are penetrating.

- I listen compassionately, intently and carefully; I recall key points and take them into account.

- I'm frank and open in my communications. I am willing to admit errors and shortcomings.

- I'm able to persuade others to give their agreement and commitment; in face of conflict, I use personal influence to achieve compromise and agreement.

- I adopt a flexible (but not compliant) style when interacting with others. I take others' views into account and am prepared to change position when appropriate.

Quick check – board performance

- We define and review the role and responsibilities of each individual director and how these contribute to the effectiveness of the board.

- Board members are effectively briefed in time to prepare for meetings.

- We regularly review the quality of the board's decisions, advice and its actions.

- The company's organisation structure and capability is appropriate for implementing its chosen strategies.

- Company objectives are consistent with the mission, values and needs of stakeholders, and form the basis of company strategy.

- The vision and mission are championed by the entire board throughout the organisation.

- The vision and mission are monitored and reviewed regularly

- Company objectives are Specific, Measurable, Achievable, Realistic and Time-bound.

- The board regularly reviews the company's Strengths, Weaknesses, Opportunities and Threats.

- The organisation's culture encourages continuous change and questioning of convention.

- The board clearly delegates authority to management and regularly reviews management's effectiveness.

- All staff, including me, receive a personal development review at least annually.

© Copyright 2017 Brefi Group Limited

5. Goal setting and review

Here is a personal development appraisal questionnaire. You should use it at least once a year. I recommend that you complete it in August as the basis for setting personal and professional development objectives for the coming year. When you have completed it you might like to discuss it with your chairman.

A key part of the process is to review your progress and achievements against the goals that you have previously set. This can be a challenge the first time round! That's why I recommend it at the beginning, before the start of your CPD year. If you are starting this programme mid-year, then set some shorter term goals so that you will have the basis for a proper review in August.

Although it refers to your job role, feel free to extend your thoughts to the whole of your career context, as well as to social and personal roles. As a director you are likely to have several job roles. The questions in italics are there to stimulate your thinking; apply them generally in the contexts that you choose.

Review

1. **How do you contribute to your organisation's objectives?**

    Briefly describe the key objectives of the organisation that relate to your role and how you can contribute to meeting them.

2. **Describe the main responsibilities of your role? Are you sure of the exact boundaries of your role?**

    Do you have a clearly defined role and contribution? Could there be opportunities for you to take more responsibility? What roles do you play, e.g. team player, advisor, coach? Do you need to seek clarification? Have you recently reviewed your role and contribution with your chairman?

3. **What strengths and weaknesses do you bring to your role?**

   For example, you might be a good communicator or a good organiser but a poor timekeeper. You might be good at big picture thinking but poor on detail. Try to identify what you are good at and also limitations where improvement would help your performance.

GOOD AT	LIMITATIONS

4. **List your main accomplishments since your last review. Have you achieved the objectives set for that period?**

   If this is your first review, list your main accomplishments in the last year.

OBJECTIVES	ACCOMPLISHMENTS

5. **Key Result Areas – you can review up to five goals here**

   1. Please list one goal you committed to achieve in the last year.

   Describe how effective you have been in achieving this?

   Wherever possible use statistics or evidence to support your description.

2. Please list one goal you committed to achieve in the last year.

Describe how effective you have been in achieving this?
Wherever possible use statistics or evidence to support your description.

3. Please list one goal you committed to achieve in the last year.

Describe how effective you have been in achieving this?
Wherever possible use statistics or evidence to support your description.

4. Please list one goal you committed to achieve in the last year.

Describe how effective you have been in achieving this?
Wherever possible use statistics or evidence to support your description.

5. Please list one goal you committed to achieve in the last year.

Describe how effective you have been in achieving this?
Wherever possible use statistics or evidence to support your description.

6. What factors within your control have affected your effectiveness?

These might be a guide to suitable development objectives to include in your personal development plan.

7. What external factors have affected your effectiveness?

Resources, communication, liaison with other departments? These might or might not apply next year, so take them into account before agreeing your objectives. They might be a guide to areas in which changes could make you more effective.

What suggestions can you make for changes that will improve the situation?

8. List examples of your personal development since your last review.

These might or might not have been a direct result of your CPD programme, or of activities or experiences in the workplace - or at home or in the community. Have you made any contribution beyond the normal call of duty? Is there anything you are particularly proud of?

© Copyright 2017 Brefi Group Limited

9.   What are your personal aspirations?

You should consider your own career aspirations but also bear in mind organisational and technical changes that could affect your future. Don't feel obliged to create aspirations that you may not have - it is quite permissible to put 'retired' or 'working elsewhere' if that answer is realistic. Think about the development consequences. Even staying in the same job role is likely to involve some activity to respond to technical and organisational change.

What would you personally like to achieve over the next 12 months?

What about longer term aspirations?

CAREER ASPIRATION   **DEVELOPMENT NEEDS**

10. What do you suggest would be suitable objectives for the next twelve months? List between three and five objectives.

Try to make your objectives specific and realistic enough for you to achieve them within a set period of time. Choose objectives that are related to improving the performance of the organisation, and the way in which you contribute to the board. If you are not sure about this, discuss it with your chairman. Please record the intended benefit.

The objectives do not have to be complicated but make sure they are in a measurable form - so that you can decide whether you have achieved them or not – they will be the basis for your review next August. And you must agree a time period for their achievement.

If you can, try to relate one of your objectives to each of the following areas (a) personal development e.g. time management, interpersonal skills; (b) organisational benefit e.g. running meetings, performance measurement; (c) technical skills e.g. finance, IT or marketing. Don't worry if you can't find objectives for each area.

OBJECTIVES	BENEFITS

11. Please make at least one suggestion for improving the effectiveness of your organisation

This is your opportunity to contribute a suggestion for improvement and to discuss it with your chairman. So don't be shy.

Personal Development Plan
CAREER ASPIRATIONS AND POTENTIAL   Time frame

Why are you absolutely committed to these goals?

Professional Development Actions

Improve key result area(s):

Objectives and Actions	Completion date

Increase personal competence(s):

Objectives and Actions	Completion date

Implement strategic change(s):

Objectives and Actions	Completion date

Career/personal development:

Objectives and Actions	Completion date

Support strategies

- Who can you add to your peer group this year to help you and assist you?

- What peer group(s) would you like to join?

- Who would you like to spend more time with?

- What daily rituals do you need to commit to?

- What do you need to stop doing?

- What newspapers, magazines, podcast should you subscribe to?

- What courses should you register for?

Commitment

Now that you have decided what to do, would you like to share it with someone? Anyway, make a formal commitment by signing below.

Signature .... *Date* ....

You can use the space below to make any further comments on how you intend to approach you continuing personal and professional development in the year ahead.

© Copyright 2017 Brefi Group Limited

CPD Record – September

This is where you record your learning and development activities. Calculate CPD points based on the 'effective learning hours' involved. Remember the process:

- Reflection – What are my needs or objectives?
- Planning – What am I going to do?
- Evaluation – What have I learned?
- Action – What have I done; how can it be applied?

Date	Activity	Outcome	Application	Points

CPD Record – October

This is where you record your learning and development activities. Calculate CPD points based on the 'effective learning hours' involved.

Remember the process:

- Reflection – What are my needs or objectives?
- Planning – What am I going to do?
- Evaluation – What have I learned?
- Action – What have I done; how can it be applied?

Date	Activity	Outcome	Application	Points

CPD Record – November

This is where you record your learning and development activities. Calculate CPD points based on the 'effective learning hours' involved.

Remember the process:
- Reflection – What are my needs or objectives?
- Planning – What am I going to do?
- Evaluation – What have I learned?
- Action – What have I done; how can it be applied?

Date	Activity	Outcome	Application	Points

CPD Record – December

This is where you record your learning and development activities. Calculate CPD points based on the 'effective learning hours' involved.

Remember the process:

- Reflection – What are my needs or objectives?
- Planning – What am I going to do?
- Evaluation – What have I learned?
- Action – What have I done; how can it be applied?

Date	Activity	Outcome	Application	Points

© Copyright 2017 Brefi Group Limited

CPD Record – January

This is where you record your learning and development activities. Calculate CPD points based on the 'effective learning hours' involved. Remember the process:

- Reflection – What are my needs or objectives?
- Planning – What am I going to do?
- Evaluation – What have I learned?
- Action – What have I done; how can it be applied?

Date	Activity	Outcome	Application	Points

CPD Record – February

This is where you record your learning and development activities. Calculate CPD points based on the 'effective learning hours' involved. Remember the process:

- Reflection – What are my needs or objectives?
- Planning – What am I going to do?
- Evaluation – What have I learned?
- Action – What have I done; how can it be applied?

Date	Activity	Outcome	Application	Points

© Copyright 2017 Brefi Group Limited

CPD Record – March

This is where you record your learning and development activities. Calculate CPD points based on the 'effective learning hours' involved. Remember the process:

- Reflection – What are my needs or objectives?
- Planning – What am I going to do?
- Evaluation – What have I learned?
- Action – What have I done; how can it be applied?

Date	Activity	Outcome	Application	Points

CPD Record – April

This is where you record your learning and development activities. Calculate CPD points based on the 'effective learning hours' involved. Remember the process:

- Reflection – What are my needs or objectives?
- Planning – What am I going to do?
- Evaluation – What have I learned?
- Action – What have I done; how can it be applied?

Date	Activity	Outcome	Application	Points

CPD Record – May

This is where you record your learning and development activities. Calculate CPD points based on the 'effective learning hours' involved. Remember the process:

- Reflection – What are my needs or objectives?
- Planning – What am I going to do?
- Evaluation – What have I learned?
- Action – What have I done; how can it be applied?

Date	Activity	Outcome	Application	Points

CPD Record – June

This is where you record your learning and development activities. Calculate CPD points based on the 'effective learning hours' involved.

Remember the process:

- Reflection – What are my needs or objectives?
- Planning – What am I going to do?
- Evaluation – What have I learned?
- Action – What have I done; how can it be applied?

Date	Activity	Outcome	Application	Points

CPD Record – July

This is where you record your learning and development activities. Calculate CPD points based on the 'effective learning hours' involved. Remember the process:

- Reflection – What are my needs or objectives?
- Planning – What am I going to do?
- Evaluation – What have I learned?
- Action – What have I done; how can it be applied?

Date	Activity	Outcome	Application	Points

CPD Record – August

This is where you record your learning and development activities. Calculate CPD points based on the 'effective learning hours' involved. Remember the process:

- Reflection – What are my needs or objectives?
- Planning – What am I going to do?
- Evaluation – What have I learned?
- Action – What have I done; how can it be applied?

Date	Activity	Outcome	Application	Points

6. Review and carry over

As your CPD year comes to an end it is time for some reflection and to identify issues to carry over into next year.

What are the main things you have learned this year?

What are you in the process of learning that needs continuing attention?

What frustrations have you encountered that suggest training/development needs?

What have you achieved in the last year? Honour yourself and identify things to celebrate ;-)

Now for a stretch!
What could be a really exciting and challenging goals for you to set for the next year and for five years?

© Copyright 2016 Brefi Group Limited

© Copyright 2016 Brefi Group Limited

The Director Development Centre

This is what we stand for...

Our Vision

Boards of directors providing strategic, moral and ethical leadership to transform the world's economy.

Mission Statement

"We help directors and boards be more effective by clarifying goals, improving communication and applying good corporate governance."

So, how can we help you?

CPD for Directors

Monthly professional development programme delivered by post:

- A4 CPD Record journal (annual)
- 48+ page CPD Guides
- CD audios with interview
- *Directors Briefing* newsletters with legal and regulatory updates, news stories and case studies.

The Essential Directorship Masterclass

- Multi-media self study programme
- Comprehensive full colour workbook
- 30+ videos (online streaming)

The New Directors Handbook

- 170 pages covering directors, boards, compliance and strategy
- Download your FREE copy of the first three chapters at: www.newdirectors.info

On-line programmes

- Webinars – occasional series covering specific issues
- Tutorial groups – private membership groups with tuition, discussion and Q&A

Live workshops

- Induction days – all you need to know for your first 100 days
- Mastermind groups - a mix of focused teaching and peer to peer support

Facilitation

- Corporate retreats, away days and strategy meetings

Find out more:
www.CorporateDirector.co.uk

www.TheDirectorsAcdemy.com

Printed by Libri Plureos GmbH in Hamburg, Germany